# MOTHER TERESA
## SISTER TO THE POOR

*The Women of Our Time® Series*

Today more than ever, children need role models whose lives can give them the inspiration and guidance to cope with a changing world. *WOMEN OF OUR TIME*, a series of biographies focusing on the lives of twentieth-century women, is the first such series designed specifically for the 7–11 age group. International in scope, these biographies cover a wide range of personalities—from historical figures to today's headliners—in such diverse fields as politics, the arts and sciences, athletics, and entertainment. Outstanding authors and illustrators present their subjects in a vividly anecdotal style, emphasizing the childhood and youth of each woman. More than a history lesson, the *WOMEN OF OUR TIME* books offer carefully documented life stories that will inform, entertain, and inspire the young people of our time.

"*Another excellent addition to the* Women of Our Time *series*"—ALA *Booklist*

"*Giff uses short sentences, wisely selected anecdotes, and pronunciation helps as she shows that one individual can change the world by helping the nearest person.*"                                                     —*School Library Journal*

# MOTHER TERESA

## SISTER TO THE POOR

BY PATRICIA REILLY GIFF

Illustrated by Ted Lewin

PUFFIN BOOKS

For Dr. John Mullee, who taught me about
"the good, the beautiful, and the true,"
for my father, William Reilly, who lived it,
and for Sister Marie Antoinette Doniaccio, D.W.,
who died for it.

P. R. G.

PUFFIN BOOKS

A Division of Penguin Books USA Inc.
375 Hudson Street, New York, New York 10014
Penguin Books Ltd, 27 Wrights Lane, London W8 5TZ England
Penguin Books Australia Ltd, Ringwood, Victoria, Australia
Penguin Books Canada Ltd, 10 Alcorn Avenue, Toronto, Ontario, Canada M4V 3B2
Penguin Books (N.Z.) Ltd, 182–190 Wairau Road, Auckland 10, New Zealand

Penguin Books Ltd, Registered Offices: Harmondsworth, Middlesex, England

First published by Viking Penguin Inc. 1986
Published in Puffin Books 1987
14  16  18  20  19  17  15

Text copyright © Patricia Reilla Giff, 1986
Illustrations copyright © Ted Lewin, 1986
All rights reserved
"Women of Our Time" is a registered trademark of Viking Penguin Inc.

Printed in U.S.A.
Set in Garamond #3

Library of Congress Cataloging in Publication Data
Giff, Patricia Reilly.     Mother Teresa, sister to the poor.
(Women of our time)
Summary: A biography emphasizing the early years of the nun who is world renowned for her work
with the poor, sick, and uneducated in India and in other parts of the world.
1. Teresa, Mother, 1910–     —Juvenile literature.   2. Nuns—India—Calcutta—Biography—
Juvenile literature.
3. Calcutta (India)—Biography—Juvenile literature.
[1. Teresa, Mother, 1910–     .  2. Nuns]   I. Lewin, Ted, ill.
II. Title.   III. Series: Women of our time (Puffin Books)
[BX4406.5.Z8G54  1987]     271'.97  [B] [92]     86-30408     ISBN 0-14-032225-6

*Special thanks to June Klippel and Kamala Dorai*

# Contents

# 1

# "I Must
# Do Something"

It was summertime, wartime.

In Beirut, Lebanon, thirty-seven children were caught in the war. They huddled on the hospital floor in the heat. Some of them were mentally retarded, some were sick. Most of them couldn't walk.

Bombs had shattered the windows, blown away a corner of the hospital. The children could hear the guns, smell the smoke.

Then above the noise was another sound, the sound of motors. Four trucks with red crosses painted on the sides braked to a stop in front of the hospital.

A moment later a wrinkled little woman with a wide grin stood in the midst of the children. She hugged the younger ones, shook hands with the older ones, then scooped up one of the babies.

Within minutes all the children were in the trucks. They sped across the country toward the green line that marked the end of the fighting, the line that meant they were safe in east Beirut.

Later, when the children had been washed and fed and tucked into clean beds, this woman was asked how she had managed to get them out.

She squinted up at the reporters. "We had the permission of everyone," she said, "the whole world."

The whole world knows this nun who was not much bigger than the tallest of the children she had rescued. Her name: Mother Teresa.

Forty years before, when she dragged a dying woman away from the filthy streets of Calcutta to wash and comfort, and started a home for the dying, people said she was mad. But she went on caring for the poor, pulling newborn babies off garbage heaps, until all India knew her, then all the world.

Indian children call this stooped little woman with large brown eyes and man-sized hands Ma, or Mother. Others call her the Saint of Calcutta, the Mother of the Poorest of the Poor.

She says she goes where she is needed. She goes without money, without comfort, owning only the two white-and-blue saris she wears, a bucket for washing, and a mat for sleeping.

It would be hard to guess how many babies she has saved, how many children she has taught, how many sick people she has nursed.

It all began because she wanted to do something, because she said, "I must do something."

In the early 1900s Skopje (say it like "Sko-pee-ay"), the capital city of Macedonia, was ruled by the Turks. It was a city of tiny ribbon streets of cobblestones, a city of carpet making and embroidery.

It was a place of round-topped mosques. There criers would climb to the top of needle-thin minarets to call the Muslims to prayer. It was also a place of churches—but low churches, churches hugging the ground. This was because the Turks had ruled that no church could be higher than the houses.

Skopje was the home of colorful gypsies as well as Turks. Greeks and Slavs and white-capped Albanians lived there, too. It was a land of mixed peoples and languages and religions.

It was the place where Mother Teresa was born.

Nikola and Drana Bojaxhiu (say it like "Bóy-ya-jeeoo") were Albanians. Shortly after 1900 they came from the city of Prizren to settle in Skopje.

They had five children. First was Age, a girl, then a son, Lazar. Then on August 26, 1910, another girl was born.

The next day an Albanian priest poured water over her forehead and placed a grain of salt in her mouth. She was baptized, brought into the church, with two names: Gonxha ("Gohn-ja"), or flower bud in Albanian, and Agnes for lamb.

Two more children would be born—and die soon after.

Drana, their mother, was a quiet Catholic woman. She took pride in taking care of her three children and keeping house.

Nikola, the father, was a patriot. He banded together with other Albanians and talked about the time when all Albanians would be united in one country. Outgoing, he filled the brick house near the Vardar River with talk and laughter and with friends who thought as he did.

Times were good for the Bojaxhiu family. Nikola was a contractor. He and an Italian friend were partners. They built many buildings. One of them was the Skopje Theater.

Agnes, the youngest, grew up beside her older sister, Age, the serious student who would become a

journalist, and her brother, Lazar, who looked forward to an army career.

Lazar called her a rosebud. He said she was "plump and round and tidy." Her face and rather long nose were very much like her mother's. Years later he remembered that she was also like her mother in her love for the church and in caring for the poor.

Until she was ten, Agnes spent happy days in school and in church, or reading and laughing with friends. Then everything changed.

One night Nikola went to a political meeting. He hoped that an area called Kosovo, where many Albanians lived, could become part of Albania. He wanted to help it to happen. When he came home from the meeting, he was sick. His family rushed him to the hospital, but it was too late.

Filled with grief, his family wondered about his death. Had it happened because of his patriotism? The political meetings he always attended? Had he been poisoned?

Now the business was gone, and so was Nikola's laughter.

Drana, whom the children called Nana Loke, mother of the soul, would have to carry on alone. Somehow she had to keep the family together, to bring back the happiness they had had.

She turned to what she knew—embroidery. She

started a small business. There was still time left to attend to her religion, her family, her house.

She insisted on discipline. She wanted the children to grow up strong and serious. One night when the three children were laughing and being silly, she shut off the electricity. The room suddenly became dark. Drana told them she would not waste electricity on nonsense.

Religion was the tie that held the family together. The morning started with Mass down the street at the Church of the Sacred Heart. Sharing in the ceremony that was most important to Catholics, where bread and wine were consecrated, made holy, was a beautiful way to start the day. It made the family feel closer.

In the afternoon they went back to church for many hours. At home they ended the day with the saying of the rosary. They knelt, fingering the beads, praying the "Our Father," the "Hail Marys."

Drana and the children became involved in prayer groups and in working with the poor. Drana taught them that the poor were part of the family, too. People who needed food or a bed for the night were welcome at their house. Even a woman who was dying of a tumor was taken in.

Agnes, who had a lovely voice, became part of the church choir. She sang alone at Christmas and took part in plays. She also joined the Sodality of Mary.

This church group had been formed hundreds of years before. Its members learned about missionaries sent to foreign lands. They wanted to help the poor through prayers and money.

When Agnes was fifteen, some Yugoslav priests set out for the missions in India. One of the priests wrote letters to the sodality. He spoke of the slums—bustees the Indians called them. He wrote of the poor, the sick, the orphans. Agnes was absorbed by his stories. She began to think about being a nun. At first she put it out of her mind, but the thought kept coming back.

Agnes prayed for a long time, until she was sure what God wanted. She believed He was calling her, telling her what to do.

She listened carefully to the stories told by missionaries who visited the church, and she pored over maps of India until she knew exactly where the missions were. They became real to her.

By the time Agnes was eighteen, she had heard of Loreto.

The Sisters of Loreto had been started by a woman named Mary Ward in the 1600s. Mary had wanted to teach others not only the usual school subjects but also about religion. Now, hundreds of years later, the Sisters of Loreto were doing this work in many parts of the world. One of the places was India.

It was the right choice for Agnes. She knew she

had to join this strict order of nuns, an order that spent hours praying and hours teaching. Her mother's teaching and that of the priests had helped prepare her for this life.

There was a problem, though. The Sisters of Loreto weren't based in Skopje. Their mother house, or headquarters, was in Ireland, a country that was far away, a damp, cold land very different from Agnes's warm Skopje.

That was where she'd have to go first—to Rathfarnum, Ireland.

But what about her family? Lazar was gone. He had already started his army career. Her mother and Age would be alone. How could she leave them? And how could she leave the brick house on the river, her friends in the choir and the sodality, her teachers, the church people?

She'd never come home again. She'd never see all those dear faces again.

But the pull toward India was strong. In her heart she knew that she had a vocation, a call from God, to be a nun.

Once she had made up her mind, once she was sure God was leading the way toward the Loreto Sisters, she never looked back.

"It was the will of God," she said. "It was His choice."

# 2

# To Follow God's Way

"I wanted to be a missionary," Mother Teresa remembered years later. "I wanted to go out and give the life of Christ to the people."

First she had to tell her family that she had made up her mind to do this. She wrote to Lazar.

He was shocked. "How could you become a nun? Do you realize that you are burying yourself?" he wrote.

Immediately she wrote back to him. "You think you are so important, as an official serving the king of two million subjects. Well, I am an official too, serving the King of the whole world."

Then it was time to tell her mother.

When Nana Loke heard the news, she knew that she'd never see Agnes again. She was heartbroken, but she too believed that God was calling her daughter.

She went to her bedroom and stayed there for the entire day. The next morning she came out and quietly began to prepare Agnes for the long trip.

Weeks later, in September, after a farewell party with the family and people from church, Nana Loke and Age took Agnes to the Skopje station. As the train pulled away, Agnes looked back at her mother and sister for the last time. Waving and crying, she watched until she couldn't see the station anymore.

Then she faced forward for the trip that would take her all the way across Europe to Paris and the ship that would take her to Ireland.

From the moment she reached the huge stone abbey of the Loreto Sisters, almost everything was strange and new.

Now Agnes was a postulant—another new word that meant knocking on the door.

In her postulant's dress, or habit as it was called, she huddled in the cold dampness of the stone building. She had to learn to eat the odd food of the Irish and to twist her tongue around a new language. In the few weeks she'd be there, Sister Borgia, a former

missionary sister, would have to teach her enough English so she'd be able to talk with the sisters and the people in India. She had to learn about the silence, too.

In the hallways she'd have to walk as softly as the other sisters. In the dining room there was no conversation the way there had been at home. One of the sisters would read aloud from the Bible or from books about the lives of the saints. The others would eat quietly, listening and making signs for what they needed at the table.

Most important was the Great Silence, the silence that was never broken at night. It was a silence that gave the sisters time to think about Mass and Communion they would receive early the next morning.

But some things about the new life were the same. In the chapel the priests wore the same vestments as they did in Skopje. And the Latin language of the Mass was exactly as she had heard it all her life. *Introibo ad altare Dei*—"I will go unto the altar of God"—the same familiar words to strengthen her resolve that she was following the way God had set for her.

Agnes stayed in the Mother House of Loreto for only six weeks. It was such a short period that years later she hardly remembered it. The sisters in Ireland didn't remember her either except as a quiet young postulant who was learning English.

13

Late in the fall of 1928 she boarded another ship. It took her from the Irish cold toward the beautiful city of Darjeeling in India. This new land wasn't flat and gray. Nestled under the snowy Himalaya Mountains, it was warm, a resort city.

India. At last she was in the mission country. Now she was a novice, a new sister. Her preparation for her religious life would really begin. She had to study the Bible, the rule of the Sisters, and the lives of the saints.

Her teachers spoke in English, the books she learned from were in English, and she was surrounded by English-speaking people. At the same time, she began to study Hindi and Bengali. When she was not studying, she was teaching children in the little one-room school on the convent grounds.

It was a new world for Agnes. As a Loreto novice she learned to treat her sisters equally. It was against the rule to love one more than another. There would be no special friendships. She was a member of a big group now, working together with the others for Christ. She was to put away thoughts of herself and to ignore her own wishes for comfort. She would be detached from the world as she had known it before. She had to have permission to leave the convent grounds, and another sister would have to go with her as a partner.

On May 4, 1931, when she was almost twenty-one

years old, she was ready to make her first profession.

Profession day was a holy day, a milestone in her life. First were the three vows she took: poverty, that she'd own nothing of her own, no money, no clothes, no jewelry; chastity, that she'd be pure in mind and body; and obedience, that she'd obey the will of her superiors in the order without question.

Next she put a thin gold circle on the third finger of her right hand. For her, this ring meant that she would never be the wife of an ordinary man. It was a symbol that she was the bride of Christ.

It was time to give up her old self, to give up Gonxha Agnes Bojaxhiu. She'd have to choose a new name, the name of a saint to guide her. She chose Mary, which all sisters did, to honor the Mother of Christ, and Teresa, the name by which she'd be known.

Two Teresas have been especially dear to Catholics. The Big Saint Teresa was a Spanish nun who lived five hundred years ago. Bold and daring, she founded an order of Carmelites.

The other Teresa was one of those Carmelite nuns. She had died as a young woman, unknown, in a small city in France, a few years before Agnes was born.

This nun, "The Little Flower" as people called her, had written a diary. When it was read after her death, everyone was amazed at her goodness. She had believed in doing the smallest, most humble tasks as perfectly as she could, for the love of God. She called it "the little way."

She was made a saint just six years before Agnes's profession day.

Agnes became Teresa. "Teresa," she said, "after The Little One."

After profession it was time for the new Sister Teresa to leave Darjeeling and travel south to Calcutta.

At first, Calcutta seemed a grand city, with wide roads and beautiful homes and government buildings. But many of the people were very poor.

These people lived in the railroad station, in drain pipes, in the gutters. During the monsoon rains they had to wade through filthy water in the streets. Many of them were horribly crippled or sick or dying. Animals and children wandered through the crowds, uncared for, starving. Smoke from broken-down cars and cooking fires made the air hazy.

The peaceful silence that Sister Teresa was beginning to love was not to be found in Calcutta. For above all the chaos was the noise of shouting, begging, and crying.

Although Sister Teresa had hoped to work with the poor, her superiors assigned her to St. Mary's Entally. This Catholic school was an oasis, a place of peace in the middle of the poverty and smells of the Moti Jheel ("Mo-tee Jeel") Slum.

Here Sister Teresa would teach geography and history to the rich Bengali girls.

Later she would say, "I taught geography for many years, but I never thought I would visit so many of the places I taught about."

The years passed quietly, every day the same. Sister Teresa would be up early to pray and to read the Scriptures. She'd attend Mass and receive Communion. Many hours would be spent with the girls, teaching; then again night prayers would end the day.

In 1937 she traveled back to Darjeeling to make her final vows. This time the three vows she made were for life. Now she was truly a Loreto Sister.

She continued to teach. She loved teaching. She loved the girls, and the girls loved her. "She taught religion in such a wonderful way," one of her pupils said, "that everything came alive for us." Another remembered, "When we were ill, she stayed up to be our nurse."

She became the principal of St. Mary's. She also became the superior of the Daughters of St. Anne, a group of Bengali sisters who taught there.

But something was wrong. This happy, quiet life was not the life she had expected. She had traveled all those miles to work for the poor. But here she was inside this beautiful stone building with the lovely, peaceful lake in front of it.

The high walls hid most of the horror outside. But from her bedroom window Sister Teresa could still see the tin roofs of the poor, the cluttered streets. She could hear the crying. In her heart she knew that was where she wanted to be, where she should be.

With the help of a priest friend, she started a Sodality of Mary. It was very much like the group she had belonged to in Skopje, the sodality of her childhood.

The girls she taught were interested in helping the poor. They went with her out to the bustees, the slums. By this time she knew Bengali, Hindi, and English. She could talk to the poor in their own language. She could visit the sick at Nilratan Sakor Hospital and know what they were asking for.

Hindu and Muslim women, as well as Catholics, joined the sodality.

Sister Teresa managed to get some bandages and a few bottles of aspirin. She went out to the streets, always with a companion, to help the sick who were lying there with no money for hospital care.

One night she brought a beggar she called Granny into the convent. She fed her and put her to sleep in her own bed.

But it wasn't enough. Not nearly enough.

Mother Cenacle was her superior. She was an understanding person who could see that Sister was being pulled toward the poor. She had an idea that she thought might help.

She took twenty children from the Moti Jheel Slum and brought them inside the gates of St. Mary's. The sisters would teach and care for them.

The idea didn't work. One by one, the children sneaked away. By the end of the year only two were left.

There was just too much of a difference for the children. It had meant giving up the world they knew, a world they were part of, for the strange newness behind St. Mary's walls.

During these years India belonged to England. More and more the Indian people began to wish for their independence. A man named Gandhi became a leader. He taught them how to resist the English without being violent themselves.

Before independence could be brought about, World War II started. Without asking, the English brought the Indians into it.

Bombs fell on Calcutta. Some of the students of St. Mary's were sent to other areas of India, but the sisters stayed with the rest.

Ships were used in the war. They no longer carried food to the people in Calcutta. Outside the convent walls, throughout the state of Bengal, more than two million people starved to death. Millions more wandered around, trying to find a few grains of rice.

With the end of the war, independence was in sight. But the starving people had to face more violence. Muslims and Hindus fought over which religion would be recognized. The country was being torn in two. People began to riot, to kill each other in the streets. Again no food would be delivered.

This time even the girls who came from families with money, the girls of St. Mary's, would suffer. There were three hundred girls in Sister Teresa's charge and no way to feed them. She had to do something.

It was dangerous to go out into the streets. Shops were being set on fire. People were being stabbed and beaten to death. As a European, as a Catholic, Sister Teresa was taking a terrible risk. There was no other way. She opened the gate and didn't come back until she had found soldiers to give them rice.

September 1946 came. It was time for Sister Teresa's retreat. Thirty-six years old now, she had made this yearly visit to Darjeeling many times. Freed from her teaching duties, she would spend several days there, praying, thinking in silence. It was a time she loved.

This September she boarded the night train. As always her thoughts were of the poor, the sick, the dying, the children. As the dusty train carried her north, she could picture the peace of St. Mary's. At the same time, she could see the slums of Moti Jheel, the bustee that was named Pearl Lake after a dirty pond that lay in that area.

Moti Jheel was outside her window, but it seemed a million miles away.

"I must do something," she kept telling herself.

Then suddenly she knew.

For years she had been saying to herself that she knew where she belonged. Every time she looked out the window. Every time she stepped into Moti Jheel.

But she hadn't known how to get there.

Now, on the dusty night train, she felt that God was calling her again. He was telling her that the people outside needed her, that they would not come behind the convent walls to her. She had to go out to them.

She called this message "a call within a call." It was not a vision from God, but a strong sense of knowing what He wanted.

She would still be a sister, but a sister in a different way.

The message was crystal clear. "I was to give up even Loreto where I was very happy," she said, "and go out in the streets. I heard the call to give up all and follow Christ into the slums to serve him among the poorest of the poor."

She felt that "It was an order. I was to leave the

convent and help the poor while living among them."

But getting outside was not to be easy. She went first to a priest, a spiritual adviser. He promised he would talk to the Archbishop of Calcutta.

The Archbishop was worried. How could he send this woman outside? In addition to the poverty, religious problems were still causing fighting in Calcutta. Sister Teresa was a Western woman. Who knew what the people might do to her?

He told her that she had to wait a year before any decision would be made.

But the faith and determination that had always been hers never wavered.

It had brought her all the way from Skopje. It had made her give up her family, her friends. It had taken her to Ireland, a place she could hardly remember anymore.

A year later she asked again. By now the Archbishop had discussed her request with priests and other people in Calcutta. He had had time to think about what she wanted to do. He agreed to her plan, provided she could get permission from her order.

The General Superior of the Loreto Sisters, Mother Gertrude, gave Sister Teresa her blessing. She wrote, "If God is calling you, I give you permission with all my heart."

The permission was given for just a year—a time of trial.

Now that the time had come, Sister Teresa felt the terrible pain of separation from her sisters.

"To leave Loreto was much more difficult than to leave my family and country to enter religious life," she said later. "Loreto, my spiritual training, my work, meant everything to me."

On August 16, 1948, she took off the black veil and the habit of the Loreto Order.

She put on a simple white cotton sari, the dress of Indian women. This sari had three stripes of blue. It was cheap and familiar to the poor. She pinned a small cross to her left shoulder, and slipped into open sandals.

It was the day to leave.

Her students and the sisters were in tears. She fought back tears too as, one by one, they hugged her and the children sang songs of farewell.

Then she walked out the gates of St. Mary's.

# 3

# One Child at a Time

Sister Teresa had one more stop before she reached the streets of Calcutta. That stop was Patna ("Pot-na"), a city 240 miles away. Patna and the Medical Mission Sisters at Holy Family Hospital.

The sisters there had agreed to help Sister Teresa learn as much as she could about sickness in a short period of time.

She was given a tiny room in the hospital. From there it was just a few steps to the patients. She learned how to give an injection. She learned how to measure medicine. She washed the children and the old people and held the hands of people in pain. She even delivered a baby.

Whenever there were a few minutes, she asked questions. The sisters were glad to answer.

They knew about the types of illnesses Sister Teresa would meet in the bustees of Calcutta, diseases that had mostly disappeared in Western countries.

There was leprosy. There were intestinal worms. There were bone-softening diseases from lack of vitamins and good food.

The sisters knew the kinds of first aid that would be helpful for Sister Teresa to use.

In a few months they filled Sister's head with all the practical advice they could.

Sister Teresa confided in them. She told of her hopes for a new group of sisters, who would work with the poorest of the poor—the people of Calcutta. These sisters would go out to the people instead of staying behind walls.

She was determined that they would live like the poor. They would wear the simple white sari with the blue border. They'd eat the same food: just rice with a little salt for seasoning.

Rice and salt? The sisters were shocked. The new sisters would quickly become as sick as the poor of India on such a diet. They told Sister Teresa that the people who worked with the poor had to be strong.

They needed to be well fed and well rested.

In the years to come, Sister Teresa would remember this advice and use it.

By this time it was nearly Christmas. Sister Teresa was ready to begin her new life.

She arrived back in Calcutta on December 21, 1948. She had five rupees—worth less than a dollar—in her pocket.

She went straight to Moti Jheel. The stench of the bustee hit her in the face. She threaded her way around huge piles of human waste mixed with old corn husks. She watched the children playing on this heap of waste, the rats running back and forth, the beggars looking for a little morsel of corn to eat.

Faced with the filth, the sickness, the hunger, the numbers of people lying in the streets, where would she begin?

She began with the children.

In the middle of the bustee she found an open spot between the huts. She smoothed down a caked patch of earth and began to trace the Bengali letters with a small stick.

One by one, the slum children came to see what she was doing. At first there were only a few, but in no time there were about thirty children. They crouched on the ground beside her.

Then she began to teach them about cleanliness.

Before she began the alphabet lesson each day, she washed them with soap and water.

What a strange experience it was for them! They had hardly ever washed. Most of them had never even seen a piece of soap.

Some of her old friends from St. Mary's heard about what she was doing and came to see her. They brought things for the school with them—paper, chairs, and, more exciting, bars of soap. Sister Teresa gave the soap to the children as prizes.

She managed to get some milk, too. It was just enough to give the children a drink at lunchtime.

After school was over for the day, she would scurry around the Moti Jheel and Til-Jala ("Teel-Jella") bustees. Someone gave her some medical supplies so she could set up a dispensary—a place to work with the sick, to give out medicine. She cleaned the sick and cared for them, bandaging them when she could get bandages. She used the knowledge she had gained and pure common sense as well.

Sometimes she begged for scraps of food at the door of the church so she could feed one or two starving people. At the same time, she continued to live the life of a sister.

Up at four-thirty in the morning, she attended Mass and received Communion. She said her prayers with the Little Sisters of the Poor, who were also working in Calcutta. She continued to pray as she taught and worked with the sick and the dying, long into the evening hours.

But for every beggar who sipped the water she brought, there were thousands more who were thirsty. For every starving man who received a scrap of food from her, there were dozens more at her feet who held their hands up for something.

For every child she taught, there were untold numbers who would never learn to read and write.

People followed her in the streets, begging for help. Those who couldn't walk clutched at her feet and the bottom of her sari.

The work she had started was endless. She was tired; every part of her ached.

She remembered the silence of Loreto that she loved, the peace. She remembered that the Mother Superior had told her that she was loved, that she could come back to the Sisters of Loreto. She wrote what she felt:

> *Today I learned a good lesson. The poverty of the poor is so hard. When I was going and going till my legs and arms were paining, I was thinking how they have to suffer to get food and shelter. Then the comfort of Loreto came to tempt, but of my own free choice, my*

*God, and out of love for You, I desire to remain.*
*Give me courage.*

She was determined. She would not stop. Instead of thinking of the crowds, the thousands, she thought of the one—the one closest, the one she was helping.

Asked how she was able to do it, how she was able to stand the terrible smell of human waste and vomit, the sickness, the dying, she said that every time she worked with someone ill, she felt as if she were meeting God.

Every time she gave someone a cup of water, she was giving it to the Lord; every time she found a scrap of food for someone, she was finding it for Him.

"We meet the Lord who hungers and thirsts in the poor," she said, "and the poor could be you or I or any person."

Up to this time she had been staying with the Little Sisters of the Poor. She wanted to be closer to Moti Jheel, closer to the people she was helping.

A priest friend helped her find a place—the upstairs room of a house owned by a Catholic teacher, Michael Gomes. Mr. Gomes not only gave her the room; he gave it to her without rent, and he made sure there was enough food for her to eat. She added a small chair, a box for a desk, and hung a picture of the Blessed Mother on the wall.

Then more help arrived for the poor in the form of a small, pretty Bengali girl named Shubashini Das ("Shu-ba-shi-nee").

Shubashini had been one of Sister Teresa's pupils at St. Mary's. Now she had graduated. She was there to help, there to stay.

Sister Teresa warned her that it would not be easy. In fact it would be terribly hard. Remembering the sisters' advice at Patna, she told Shubashini that she would have enough to eat—but just enough. She would have to give up her lovely saris, her home, her family. She would have to give them up willingly . . . and with love.

The shy Shubashini, smaller even than Sister Teresa, nodded. She became Sister Teresa's first postulant. She put on the plain white sari that cost about a dollar. She pinned the small crucifix to her left shoulder, and she took a new name.

Shubashini was now Sister Agnes, Agnes in honor of Sister Teresa's own baptismal name. Next came the new Sister Gertrude, and Sister Bernard, and Sister Frederick.

They would soon learn that Sister Teresa was fiercely determined to reach out to the poor. They would live like the poor; otherwise she would never be able to face them. There would be no fans in the stifling hot rooms, no extra food, no extra rest.

From morning to night they would work with the poor. As a matter of fact, instead of the usual three vows a nun takes—poverty, chastity, and obedience—they would take four. This fourth one would be a promise to serve the poorest of the poor.

On October 7, 1950, the Archbishop said the first Mass at the Gomes house. Sister Teresa was given permission to go on with the work. It was the beginning of the order of sisters she had hoped for. She called them the Missionaries of Charity . . . and from then on she would be called Mother.

Now more of Mother Teresa's old students arrived. They began to crowd into the top floor of Michael Gomes's house on Creek Lane.

Soon Mr. Gomes had to build another bathroom. He had to close in areas on the roof for showers. He was happy to do it. "We received," he said. "We did not give."

In the meantime these new sisters joined Mother Teresa in church at four-thirty every morning. Barefoot, they knelt on the stone floor to pray.

Then they went out on the street. They went from door to door, asking for food for the poor. Sometimes they were refused; sometimes they'd come away with a small basket of food.

Now there were ten of them, and more coming. They lived together on the upper floor, "sleeping side by side like sardines," as a friend said.

Soon Mother Teresa realized that no matter how poorly they might want to live, there truly was not enough room in the house of Michael Gomes.

She began to pray for a bigger place. She began to look. She walked through the streets hoping for something to turn up.

Priests in the area were looking, too. They heard about a man who was leaving Calcutta. This man was a Muslim. He went to a mosque to pray. The priests told him about the sisters. He said he would give his house to Mother Teresa. "I got that house from God," he said. "I give it back to Him."

Mother had only to pay for the land on which it stood, and the Archbishop lent her the money to do it.

In February 1953 she moved the sisters into their new home. Its address, 54A Lower Circular Road, was to become famous all over the world.

# 4

# Love Until It Hurts

In Calcutta there is a Hindu temple. It is known as Kalighat ("Ka'-li-gat"). It is dedicated to Kali, the goddess of death.

Kali is pictured as a statue made of black stone. Her tongue of gold hangs down over her chin, and her body is covered with gifts of jewelry from the faithful Hindus who visit her.

While Mother Teresa was still living at Mr. Gomes's house, she was looking for a new place, a place to shelter the dying.

It was in a pair of rooms in the rear of Kalighat

that she found it. She called it Nirmal Hriday ("Nirmul Hree-day"), the Place of the Immaculate Heart.

Mother Teresa's wish to open a house for the dying began with a woman she found in front of a hospital. This woman was in miserable condition. She was caked with dirt. Rats and ants had bitten at her legs and feet.

Mother Teresa half-carried, half-dragged her inside. The people in the hospital didn't want to keep her.

Hindus believe that everything a person suffers is meant to be. That is his karma ("car-muh"). A person pays for the evil he has done in an earlier life by suffering in this life. The punishment may be sickness, poverty, or bad luck. Since there is nothing a person can do about it, he accepts it, and so does everyone else.

The hospital staff had no idea how stubborn Mother Teresa was. She told them that they had to take the woman. She'd stay until they did.

At last they took the woman in.

Mother Teresa went straight to the city hall. She needed a place, she said, a place where the dying could die, not like animals, but loved and clean and cared for.

The town officials agreed. There were those rooms, the ones in back of Kalighat. Years before, they had been used for Hindu travelers. When they came to

37

worship Kali, they would rest in the back rooms. But now travelers didn't use it anymore. No, now it was a hangout for drug addicts and gamblers. Mother Teresa could have it. She was overjoyed.

The place was dirty. It would probably take months to clean it up. But that was not good enough. Mother needed it immediately. She and the sisters set to work to clean it.

As soon as it was ready, a week or so later, they were out on the streets, dragging the dying out of the gutters.

At first there were no beds in the house, but that didn't stop the sisters. They laid the dying carefully on the black marble floor.

Even though they were faced with dreadful sights and smells, they were encouraged by Mother Teresa's words: "See God in everyone you meet."

The sisters' faces were warm and loving as they washed the dying, as they removed maggots from their wounds, as they gave water or soup to them.

"They are Jesus," Mother Teresa said of the dying. She made sure that her sisters bent close to them as they worked, holding their hands, patting their shoulders.

Nearby neighbors began to complain. Their view of the dying was different from the Catholic view.

Why were the nuns caring for the sick? They could

not change a person's karma or keep his soul from passing into a new body when he died. Did they want to make them Catholics? It was against Indian law for a person to try to change someone's religion.

The people didn't know that the dying died as they had lived. For the Catholics, there were the Last Rites of the Church. For the Muslims, sisters read from their holy book, the Koran. For the Hindus, they sprinkled precious water from the Ganges on their lips.

Some of the Hindus began to chase the sisters. They threw sticks. Then a group of men even entered the House of the Dying. They surrounded Mother Teresa and told her they were going to kill her.

She shrugged. Killing her would just send her to heaven. They backed away and left.

Then the neighbors sent a policeman to remove Mother from the temple. He stood there watching Mother clean dreadful wounds with love. He saw her care, her kindness.

He shook his head. Unless the town people would ask their own mothers and sisters to come to the temple and care for the sick, he would not make Mother Teresa leave.

The town people continued to grumble. Mother Teresa continued to carry the dying into the temple.

One of those people had a disease called cholera.

No one would touch him. No hospital would take him. Everyone was terrified of getting cholera, too.

Mother Teresa picked the man up herself. She brought him into the House of the Dying. She washed and cared for him until he died.

Then the people of the town learned that he was a Hindu. Not only was he a Hindu, but he was a Hindu priest. He had worked at the Kalighat temple before he had become ill.

Suddenly people changed their attitude toward Mother Teresa.

Neighboring women came into the House of the Dying to help. Working people came before they went to work. They'd help the sisters clean one or two of the sick, or spoon some dal—beans ground up into a broth—into a sick woman.

Doctors came, too, when they could. They helped diagnose illnesses and suggest treatment.

Help came in the way of needed supplies. Drug companies began to donate medicines. People gave old clothes, extra food. Someone sent some canvas mattresses and some small, flat pillows.

One woman, Ann Blaikie, wanted to help Mother Teresa, too. She began to gather old clothes for Mother's poor. She organized her friends, and they became known as Co-Workers. Eventually people from all over the world were signing up as Co-Workers to help in Mother Teresa's work.

Mother Teresa had not forgotten the children, though. The school at Moti Jheel had continued and was growing. But what about the orphans? Some of them were children of the people who had died in Kalighat. What about the children of the poor . . . children who were starving to death in front of their mothers' eyes? What about the children who were thrown out, unloved, on top of the garbage heaps?

By 1955 Shishu Bhavan ("Shee'-shu Bah-ven") was opened.

Shishu was a building not far from the Mother House on Lower Circular Road. It was unpainted, with crayoned drawings and words splashed across the walls. But Mother Teresa was glad to get it.

As soon as they had cleaned it, Mother Teresa and the sisters went out to the streets and the garbage dumps to pick up the abandoned babies and children.

Some of the babies were less than a day old. Many of them who were brought into Shishu lived for only an hour or so. They were just too small or just too sick to survive. But those who died were clean, and they had been held and loved by the sisters.

That was what Mother Teresa wanted. "Person to person," she called it. She was not a social worker out to reform the whole world. She did not want to become involved in politics. She wanted to see God in each person.

Now some of the babies were saved. Even the very little ones who were no bigger than a grown-up's hand somehow managed to survive. Mother dressed them in green-and-white-checked clothing small enough for dolls and placed them lovingly in boxes, in packing crates, or gently on the floor. They were cared for by smiling sisters who were as young as sixteen, as old as seventy.

Mother began to think about the children's future. They had to be raised, and, most of all, they had to find the love of a family. She began to look into the possibility of having these children adopted—in India if possible, but if not, in Europe, or even the United States.

For those who couldn't be placed, there was still a home at Shishu Bhavan. The sisters would be their family.

But there were so many children. And so many things they needed.

Mother Teresa always worked with the closest one. She tried not to think about the others; otherwise she never would have been able to manage.

Whatever the sisters did had to be done with joy and laughter. "Go back to bed," she told one sister who seemed sad.

She wrote a memo for the blackboard in the Mother House. It said: "I prefer our sisters to make mistakes through kindness than to perform miracles through harshness."

And now more and more people were beginning to notice what Mother Teresa was doing. They called her mad, they said she was crazy, but they came to help anyway.

Some came with money. "I want you," she said, "not your money." She told them to give of themselves until it hurt . . . but then it wouldn't hurt anymore.

Still the people came, and so did the money.

Mother Teresa knew how to use it all. She was an Indian citizen herself now. She knew Indian culture as well as she had known Albanian culture. Better perhaps.

She knew, for example, that a boy needed school. Not her Moti Jheel schooling . . . that was a slum school not recognized by the Indian government. No, if a boy was to stay out of the slum, he had to have a recognized education.

This education was not so important for a girl. A poor Indian girl stayed home to care for the younger children. What she needed was a dowry. Without it no man would marry her.

This dowry was a gift to the groom to start the new couple in their married life. Even if the dowry was only a sari, a wedding ring, a few odds and ends of furniture, it had to be found.

When people came to Mother and asked how they could help, she told them. Sponsor a child. Give a little money each month.

The girls would get their dowries. The boys would get their education.

She thought of another plan, too. Suppose people sponsored a child who still lived with his poor family, perhaps the oldest or the brightest. If even one of a family was educated, then the rest of the family could survive with his help.

She sent the sisters to marriage brokers, people who found husbands and wives for her growing children. This was the accepted way in India. Often a bride and groom had never seen each other before the wedding.

She made sure that Hindu children were engaged to Hindus, Muslim children to Muslims, and Christians to Christians.

She even found material, sheer and lovely, for wedding gowns, and held the wedding receptions there in Shishu Bhavan, with cakes and sweets.

Shishu became a center for many activities. When Mother found boys out on the street in the late afternoon, she asked what they were doing. Learning to steal and rob, was the reply. She opened a late-afternoon high school to keep them off the streets.

She started a food line and gave rice and bananas to those who needed them. One night, when that wasn't enough, she handed the sisters' dinner plates out the door of the Mother House.

She began to think about these beggars. She had seen so many people covered with rags from head to toe, sitting in the streets asking for food. These people looked like bundles of old rags. They didn't get much help, though. They were shunned. They were told to get out of the streets. The reason? Leprosy.

Leprosy is an old disease, a feared disease. In the days of the Bible lepers had to carry a bell and call out, "Unclean, unclean," when someone came near. In India feelings about leprosy hadn't changed. If leprosy was a person's karma, then he must have a hard lesson to learn from a past life.

People were desperately afraid of catching the disease. They feared the thickening of the skin, the loss of feeling. They were terrified of losing fingers and toes, ears, the nose.

Called by its correct name, Hansen's disease, it was less frightening. People in the West were not worried about it anymore. They knew that the disease was not as contagious as people believed. It rarely spread, except in hot climates where people were crowded together.

In the slums of India, of course, the conditions were

47

more likely to help in the spread of the disease. And uneducated people were terrified. But there was a treatment that was especially effective if given early enough, before the disease affected nerve endings.

Lepers were afraid to say they had the disease, though. They knew they would lose their jobs and even their families. They hid the disease as long as they could—until they lost part of a finger, or until the condition showed on their faces, until someone else in the family had leprosy, too.

Mother Teresa wanted to tackle that problem next. She began to look for a place for a leper colony.

The first place she found was a spot of land between the railroad tracks. The local people found out about what she had in mind. When she went to look at the property, they threw stones. She told her sisters they'd have to go somewhere else. She had to do something. There were more than two million lepers in India, and more than thirty thousand in Calcutta alone.

Then something wonderful happened. A priest, the Reverend Alfred Schneider, head of Catholic Relief Services in Delhi, wanted to give something to Mother, a personal gift from himself.

What did she want?

She wanted an ambulance, a medical van that could go from place to place.

Schneider gave her twenty-five hundred dollars,

Catholic Relief Services gave her the rest, and an American electric company sent money to be used for lepers.

Part of her problem would be solved with this ambulance. If she couldn't have the lepers in one spot, she could go to them. The ambulance could go out from Shishu Bhavan every day and treat lepers in their own communities.

Work started in 1957. "Touch a leper," Mother told her sisters. "Touch him with love." To those lepers who had already lost a finger or a hand, to those who could no longer work at their jobs, the sisters began to teach new trades. The lepers learned how to make shoes, to weave cloth, to make bandages.

The sisters pounded away at the idea: come early. Come when you have just one spot of leprosy and you can be cured.

Mother Teresa finally found a place for these lepers who needed to be in a sheltered community. Shanti Nagar ("Shan'-tee Nah'-ger"), the Place of Peace, was a place of small houses, with trees and a pond. Lepers in advanced stages of the disease could live and die among friends.

Mother Teresa was still not satisfied. There was a whole world outside, a world of sick, a world of poor, millions of sad, unhappy people.

She wanted to do more.

# 5

# Mother of the World

Fifteen years had passed since Mother Teresa had walked out on the street alone. She kept on working. Even when she was sick, she continued to care for others. She had no patience for her own illness.

Once when she broke her arm, it had to be bandaged tightly to her body. Having her arm confined was impossible. She had one of the sisters take the bandage off.

There were so many who needed her. So many that some people said that what she was doing was only a drop in the bucket. The poor still lived in the streets, the children still starved. They said Mother Teresa should be trying to do something to change the system. She should be involved in politics, in changing the government.

She refused to allow herself to think about that. She was not a social worker. "I never care for a crowd," she said, "only for one person." She continued to pick up the nearest one to her, to work at what was at hand.

Her back became stooped. The lines around her eyes and mouth deepened. Her skin became leathery from the hot Indian sun.

Young women flocked to her. The Mother House on Lower Circular Road didn't seem so huge anymore. Now the sisters were sleeping two and three to a room. They slept on mattresses on the floor; they even slept on the dining room table.

Mother Teresa was convinced that no matter how big the order grew, her sisters must be able to live like the poor.

She set up rules for them. New applicants had to join the sisters to work for six months before they could be admitted to the Missionaries of Charity as postulants. The work was hard and heartbreaking. Not everyone would have the stamina to work in the House of the Dying or in Shishu or with the lepers.

Not only did the new sisters have to have strength

and good health; they had to have a good disposition. Mother Teresa enjoyed a joke. She wanted her sisters to laugh, too. She wanted them to meet the poor with a smile. "It's the beginning of love," she said.

As word got around that Mother was performing what amounted to miracles, more volunteers came, men as well as women.

In 1963 Mother set up the Missionary Brothers of Charity. The brothers used their strong arms to carry the sick and dying; they used their warmth and love to help with the men and young boys.

Then suddenly Mother Teresa became famous. The Pope visited India and was given a white Lincoln Con-

tinental car for his trip. When he left, he gave the car to Mother Teresa for her work. Of course, she would never ride around in such a car.

She raffled it off and was able to get thousands of rupees for it. This money would go to Shanti Nagar, her new settlement for lepers.

Then requests began to pour in. Would Mother Teresa come to Delhi and Bombay to open houses? And to Venezuela, Rome, and Tanzania? Would she open a place in Australia for the aborigines? In Harlem for the poor? In Belfast for the needy?

Mother was able to do what seemed impossible. Wherever the poor were, there were the Missionaries of Charity.

Mother Teresa would send six or seven sisters to open a house. One of them would be the Superior, in charge of the others. They would find a place, roll up their sleeves, and clean it up. Soon a tiny school existed, or a place to treat the sick.

Sometimes they opened houses in dangerous areas. Once the sisters called Mother from Amman, Jordan, and told her that there was a civil war. She asked them whether they wanted to stay. When they told her yes, she was pleased and joked, "Call me up when you are dead."

Now Mother spent time going from convent to convent. Wherever she went, she asked for food. "I'll take it with me," she'd say.

She gathered together the food and the old clothing. When the airline officials refused to take the half-tied packages, she knelt in the airport and prayed until they changed their minds.

All the flying was expensive. Yet she needed to go to her different orphanages, her schools. And she had no money. Could she work as a stewardess to pay for her passage? she asked the people at the airlines.

Indira Gandhi, the prime minister, was horrified when she heard of Mother's request. Mother Teresa was not only the mother of Calcutta, she was the mother of India. From then on, Mother traveled free anywhere in the world on Air India.

She loved the flights. She was able to sit in silence, quietly saying her rosary.

Prizes began to pour in. She received a prize from the president of India and the Magsaysay Award for International Understanding from the Philippines. She was awarded the Pope John XXIII Peace Prize and dozens of honorary degrees from universities all over the world.

She didn't care about the prizes; she hated to speak in public. She made herself do it, though. The prizes gave her money for the poor; the speeches gave her a chance to talk about her belief in God.

In 1979 wonderful news came. The Nobel Peace Prize was to be given to the sixty-nine-year-old Mother Teresa. It was the world's greatest honor, with the biggest prize money: $190,000.

All India was wild with joy. The newspapers reported: "The Mother of Bengal has become the Mother of the World."

Mother Teresa spent the next few days trying to escape the cameras, the well-wishers, the excitement. "I am unworthy," she said.

Days later she went to Oslo, Norway. Over her sari she wore a threadbare coat. She was on her way to accept the prize, to speak in front of kings and other leaders of the world.

She had a message, she told a friend. It was the

same message she had thought about for all the years since she was a young girl.

"I will say, 'Love one another as God loves each one of you.' " She smiled, creasing the lines in her face.

By this time, her sisters were working in more than sixty houses around the world. Her brothers had opened more than ten.

But still it wasn't enough. She kept sending her sisters to new areas. By the 1980s there were about 120 houses. She had a house in her own Skopje now, and places in the United States, in New Guinea, in South America, Africa, and all over Europe. Her brothers had expanded in many parts of the world, too. They had more than thirty houses.

Mother Teresa went on, becoming older and more fragile. It was time for her sisters to take on some of her responsibilities. "Everyone has something to give," she always said.

She divided the work among the sisters who were flocking from around the world to help. The sisters teased her, asking her what she was going to do. Her eyes twinkled. "I will be loving you," she said.

Mother Teresa continues to visit her houses, to speak at assemblies and in churches. She still has a message. Millions of poor and sick wait. She has to tell the world about them.

It was not easy to write about Mother Teresa. She is reluctant to have people write about her youth, about herself. "Talk about the work," she has told people.

Because I was taught by sisters not only in elementary school, but also in high school and college, it is not hard for me to understand Mother's philosophy. I wanted to know about my teachers, their families, and their names. They always answered that what was important was the work they did, the way they lived their lives now.

To write this book, I read about Mother and spoke with sisters. I listened to the stories of volunteers who had worked with her. I have a picture of her in my mind now . . . a woman of strength who set out alone to change things by working with just one person, the person closest to her.

She has made me realize that each one of us has the power to change things, to make the world a better place. I like to think about that. I hope my readers will, too.

P. R. G.

58